CONFIDENCE IN THE UNKNOWN

Never fear you are not alone
God is with you crushing every stone
Commanding all dark assignments to
bow to Him alone
Because we have finally come home

He has melted all our problems right
down to the bone
Breaking every stronghold that threatens
to take hold
And plant in us sadness at what life has
thrown
Exposed by all the sins we have done

He tells us that we are His own
And we will never walk alone
Because we have come and our sins are
now atoned
We will never fear the unknown

Deuteronomy 31:8
"Do not be afraid or discouraged, for the LORD will personally go ahead of you. He will be with you; he will neither fail you nor abandon you."

BELLY OF THE BEAST

From the belly of the beast
Demons move seeking clueless prey
With enticements luring them away
From the Word and how to pray

With distractions and what the world would say
Listening rather to what is at play
More than what the Master wants from you today
To be penitent and humble in every way

Seek the Lord while it is still day
No more time to wait and play
Living life on a fancy tray
Forgetting that you will eventually have to pay

1 Chronicle 16:11
Look to the LORD and his strength; seek his face always.

BROKENNESS

He sees us in our brokenness
Heals us in our empty spaces
Lights the way to Him
Relieves us of our pain and sin

Comforts when there is no one near
Listens when we call to Him
Lifts us from the ragged heap
And sets us where we need to be

Wipes away the falling tears
He opens our eyes so that we can see
The grace and beauty of God who sees
Us, as He carries and sets us free

Psalms 34:18 The LORD is nigh unto them that are of a broken heart; and saveth such as be of a contrite spirit.

RESTORATION

I felt the brokenness in my thoughts
Despised and worthless by the words
You pile on me as I battle with despair
Locked in the insecurity of my deepest fear

Till Jesus came and set me free
Healed the scars that weighed me down
Took my cross and pain for me
And told me I am His masterpiece

Now I sing of the graces I received
When I turned to look at Him
My Comforter and the shield I see
Who restored belief and hope in me

*Psalms 51:17 The sacrifices of God are a
broken spirit: a broken and a contrite heart,
O God, thou wilt not despise.*

GOD'S TIME

What can I say this is not the end
You were more than just a friend
Even though death may be the fiend
Your time has come as God intends

I bear the pain within my heart
Knowing that we are now apart
Remembering how you played your part
As a mother whose love was off the chart

May you rest in heaven above
Looking down with motherly love
On your children who are beloved
Who now rely on the memory's store

Psalms 27:14 - *Wait on the LORD: be of good courage, and he shall strengthen thine heart: wait, I say, on the LORD.*

THE LAMB THAT CAME

Blessed are those who are called by your name
To proclaim your greatness and your fame
Everlasting Prince of Peace that forever reigns
And His wonders will never seize and will always
remain

Domination belongs to you our King
Sovereign power whose authority
Has control over every living thing
Master of the whole Universe that we live in

In obedience, we worship Him
Like the angels we too sing
Of the glory of His majesty
Mighty Saviour, the Lamb that came

John 1:29 *The next day he saw Jesus coming toward him, and said, "Behold, the Lamb of God, who takes away the sin of the world!*

THROUGH THE STORM

The world is like the dark blue sea
With raging winds that hit the shores
Violent waves that suddenly calms
When the sun comes out of the storm

Are you ravaged by what you face?
Thinking that there is no escape
Wondering when the pain will finally end
And there is nothing more to
contend

Stir within you the spirit man
That lies hidden beneath the sand
Struggling to see who will give you a hand
So that you can reach the Promised land

Isaiah 41:13 *For I am the LORD your God who takes hold of your right hand and says to you, Do not fear; I will help you.*

BELIEVING IN THE DIVINE

Faith is hoping in things that are unseen
Believing not on all that is seen
Blossoming Passion in Jesus the King
Whose endless love has spared all human beings

Faith moves mountains and make molehills small
Turns woes and troubles into problems that are
solved
Igniting hope that will install
Giving you confidence that will make you stand
tall

Faith will lead you to things that are above
Open doors that once were closed
Grant you grace that is available for all
With promises that God will fulfil

Mark 11:24 Therefore I tell you, whatever you ask for in prayer, believe that you have received it, and it will be yours

WITH THE HOLY SPIRIT

Holy Spirit plant in us your Special seed
Let it blossom and on your word, we feed
Seeking Jesus who is one with you
Professing mercy and grace we see in you

Gracious Spirit we call to thee
Help us always to break free
From pain and confusion, we might feel
When we try to preach the Gospel to those we
see

Be the light that we look up to
Pushing dangers as we wage through
Life on earth as you have taught us to
Overcoming problems through our faith
in you

Romans 15:13 May the God of hope fill you with all joy and peace in believing, so that by the power of the Holy Spirit you may abound in hope."

YEARNING

Often our restless spirits yearn
To feel your presence and discern
The wonders and lessons we must learn
Before our Saviour makes His return

You are the fount of true life
Bringing joy that your love imparts
As we seek peace within our hearts
Directed to your glorious light

Psalms 42:1 *As the deer pants for streams
of water, so my soul pants for you, my God.*

TURN TO HIM

When things seem bleak,
 I turn to Him
Because He never lets me down
Always there to comfort me
And through His eyes I clearly see
There is no one I trust as much as He

Even in the darkest hour
He shields me when things turns sour
Fights for me, so there is no fear
About whom cares because He holds me dear

My faith in Him is made complete
Performing miracles that are not discrete
He tells the world that I am His
And nothing can change His plans for me

Isaiah 45:22

"Turn to Me and be saved, all the ends of the earth; For I am God, and there is no other.

THE SPIRIT'S VOICE

Do we listen to the Spirit's voice?
As He speaks gently to our soul
Open up and you will hear His call
Ministering hope as you join His fold

The Holy Spirit was left on earth
As God's true love is unearthed
To protect, guide and give us hope
Working tirelessly to expand our scope

He brings a feeling of tranquillity
Changed our fate and our fragility
Inspires us to work above our ability
Through the grace of His spiritual capability

John 14:26 **But the Helper, the Holy Spirit, whom the Father will send in my name, he will teach you all things and bring to your remembrance all that I have said to you.**

INVINCIBLE

There were times when I felt Invincible
Unprepared for the inevitable
Unaware of the things that remain invisible
Yet in time has become visible

When I thought that I had reached the end
Jesus said" I am here to defend
To save the lost, heal the sick as God intends
And do more than our minds can comprehend"

Now I sing out with the greatest praise
Because Jesus broke me from my malaise
I owe Him life, my love, my joy
Knowing that the hold of sin in me is destroyed

Psalm 136:1
*Give thanks to the Lord, for he is good, for his
steadfast love endures forever.*

KING JESUS

In His presence we proclaim
King Jesus there is no other name
That has power to take away our shame
And that is why we exclaim

King Jesus, you have arranged
Great rejoicing as we call on your name
Moving mountains and nothing remains the
same
Filling us with your Spirit, the Blazing flame

Now our lives have truly changed
And through His mercy we have obtained
 Redemption with the gift of Heaven gained
Heirs to the Kingdom as God arranged

*Ephesians 1:7 In whom we have our redemption
through his blood, the forgiveness of our
trespasses, according to the riches of his
grace.*

BLESSED SAVIOUR

Blessed Saviour, Lord of Life
Who has opened the gates to Paradise
Fought our bodies from mortal strife
Heard the humble when they cry

The Special Victim whose sacrifice
Spreads His goodness and our joy suffice
From His strength that we rely
For He is faithful and that is no lie

Let us continue in ceaseless praise
Worship Him whose body was raised
 He ascended to prepare a place
And welcome Christians onto a glorious phase

Colossians 3:17
And whatever you do, in word or deed, do
everything in the name of the Lord Jesus,
giving thanks to God the Father through him.

GIVE THANKS

Give thanks with a grateful heart
Give thanks with an open heart
For all the wonders He has done
Call him Christ the Holy One

In our weakness, He chose to die for us
Brought us life and removed the curse
Shed His blood as a price for us
And leads us on the path that is just

We are sinners that always fall
Sometimes refusing to listen to the Master's call
Now saved from the death meant for all
Living redeemed, welcomed into the saintly hall

Psalm 118:24
*This is the day that the Lord has made; let us rejoice
and be glad in it.*

FAITHFUL GOD

In my fear I look up to you Lord
There is no one that I trust but you
You are faithful and your words are true
 comforts me and makes things brand new

I am rich because I hold on to you
 Christ, the Deliverer who people run to
In His mercy, He wipes away our sins
Makes us whole and comes to dwell within

Let us praise His mighty name
The God who has taken away all our shame
Washed us clean so that we will gain
A place in Heaven where the Master reigns

Ephesians 1:18 *I pray that the eyes of your heart may be enlightened in order that you may know the hope to which he has called you, the riches of his glorious inheritance in his holy people*,

VALIANT

Loving Shepherd of thy sheep
Who always keeps His Lamb's in safety keep
Even when dangers fill your surrounds
He sends His angels and they camp around

Nothing can His power withstand
None can pluck us from His hand
He is our strength that is why we stand
Strong and valiant held in God's own hands

Psalms 91: 11" For *He will give His angels charge concerning you, to guard you in all your ways. "*

REBORN

Bread of life who was chosen
To free the world and save the broken
Offer us hope through the Word that is spoken
And spreading His love as a token

Cup of life that whose blood was shed
Paschal victim, paschal bread
Healing the sick and raising the dead
Sacrificial lamb, the Good News that has been
shared

We are reborn and our lives are renewed
As we celebrate His body in the host that is
viewed
Daily on the altar as we share in the wine
And acknowledge the power of the divine

*John 6:35 And Jesus said to them, "I am the
bread of life*

GOD'S PERFECT LOVE

Perfect Is His love for us
Never leaving even when we fuss
About the trials that put us in a rut
And we are unable to discuss
Out of fear and lack of trust

There is no one like our God
He is more than a weight in Gold
Everything the prophets told
Slowly in our lives unfold

Always near to hear to comfort when we
 call
Picks us up when we fall
Gives us peace the world believe is
unreal
Confident because we answered the
Saviour's call

1 John 4:19"We love because God first loved us."

BLESSED CORD

The just shall live by faith alone
Softened hearts and not that of stone
Broken for sins atoned
By the Sacrifice of Jesus that is known

In humility come to the Lord
Faithfully holding on to the Blessed Cord
That gave us eternal life and welcomes us
aboard
The Heavenly ship heading to a place above

Colossians 1:17 He is before all things, and in Him all things hold together. He is before all things, and in him all things hold together.

FIGHT THE GOOD FIGHT

Fight the good fight
With all your might
Doing what the Lord sees as right
So, that others may come and see your light

Wage your war against all that is dark
Pray out loud as if it is a bark
Tearing darkness around you apart
Guided by the Holy Spirit right from the start

The cohort of angels will be at your side
Helping you battle with those that incite
Pain and anguish with their evil sights
As agents bent on destruction and adding to
human plight

1 Timothy 6:12 "Fight the good fight of the faith. Take hold of the eternal life to which you were called and about which you made the good confession in the presence of many witnesses."

RENAMED

Liberated through Christ his Son
Who our hope is firmly laid on
Bringing light on which our lives
depend upon
Radiant in the grace that we rely on

Breaking hearts of stone
Where darkness is overthrown
And love is shown
So, that we never walk alone

Master, Saviour Jesus who came
And sin was slain by the power of His name
Victoriously fighting every battle that would
 have brought us shame
Setting the captives free now children of God
renamed

*Isaiah 62:2 And you will be given a new name
by the LORD's own mouth.*

PRECIOUS GIFT

I often wonder what life would be
Without the knowledge of serving Thee
Devoid of love that we know is free
Given for our sake at Calvary

Overwhelmed by the precious gift
Presented in Christ your Son
Waiting expectantly for His return
Doing what needs to be done

Called disciples to who we belong
To the God whose only Son
Was sent to die so that we are one
With the Father, Son and Holy One

*1 Corinthians 11:1 Be imitators of me,
just as I also am of Christ.*

SELF INDULGENCIES

Living life without a care
Learning that you will not share
But expect the world to be fair
Even though you exhibit a careless flair

Are you wiser as you get older?
Or simply bolder with the world on your
shoulder
Planting sparingly and you are feeling colder
When you realise all the negatives in your
folder

That is when reality sets in and you will find
That you are considered cruel and unkind
One who has lost the way that God designed
Because of self- indulgences that leaves you
behind

1 John 1:9 - If we confess our sins, he is faithful and just to forgive us [our] sins, and to cleanse us from all unrighteousness.

ACCEPTANCE

So many words left unsaid
As the silence grows and we dread
The severed thread of life now you are dead
While you proceed on the journey up ahead

The cord that held us close is no longer there
And in our loss this family shares
The grief of leaving us as we bear
That feeling of missing your gentle care

With loving memories, we let you go
Knowing that God has called you home
And you will dwell close to God's throne
Waiting till He calls your family home

Revelation 21:4. 'He will wipe every tear from their eyes.

DOORWAY

He was tempted in every way
Keeping the devil far and at bay
Understanding that He was the only way
That Salvation could be brought to man today

He is the doorway that we seek
Only through Him that we shall reach
Eternal happiness to Heaven's beach
Where God resides and angels speak

John 10:7-9 Therefore Jesus said again, "I tell you the truth, I am the gate for the sheep. All who ever came before me were thieves and robbers, but the sheep did not listen to them. I am the gate; whoever enters through me will be saved. He will come in and go out and find pasture.

CHOOSE

There is a question I need to ask
Are you on a journey that will last?
Or just a trip where you will crash
Lacking perspective and you are falling fast

It is not a race where we lay slack
Thinking only of all the things we lack
You called to spread His name
Around the world and increase His fame

He spoke in parables but to you He gave
The chance to understand what you have
An innate gift which will depart
If you fail to rise up and do your part

So, listen carefully and choose what you will do
To serve Him fervently and do what is true
Or become forgotten among the throes and
cues
Marked for death because you gave away the
grace; He gave to you

*Proverbs1: The fear of the Lord is the
beginning of knowledge, fools despise wisdom
and instruction*

REPENTING

Let us worship at His throne
Coming to the Saviour because we are one
In his likeness we become
Redeemed and washed by the Holy One

Honour and glory to our King
Let the nation's rise and gaily sing
Of the salvation that He brings
When we turn and believe in Him

No one loves us like our God
Shows His mercy and does not withhold
Grace and anointing that comes to all
That repents and follows Christ our Lord

2 Chronicles 30:9 *For the Lord your God is gracious and compassionate. He will not turn his face from you if you return to him.*

THE REMAKE

We are all Prisoners of our own device
Caught up in problems hidden under a disguise
Of worldly pleasures and different vices
Bent to confuse and entice

Wrapped in worries that take centre stage
Professing changes in this new age
While people languish inside their cage
Hoping that answers will jump off the page

Strongholds fall and mountain shake
When you go to Jesus who in His wake
Dispels anxieties and our mistakes
Gives us a chance for a remake

*1 Peter 5:7 "Cast all your anxiety on him
Because he cares for you*.

COMMISSIONED

Stand united in Christ the King
Saved, delivered from dark and sin
Now reborn, alive to worship him
Worthy vessel to be used by Him

Have the courage to preach the word
The Holy Spirit will bring great reward
Grant you strength and give you hope
Protection and grace to help you cope

You are commissioned to do his will
Love each other and do not kill
Be a neighbour to the world and kin
And let your purpose align with His

John 8:31–38. So, Jesus said to the Jews who had believed him, "If you abide in my word, you are truly my disciples, and you will know the truth, and the truth will set you free."

IMMORTAL LOVE

Immortal love that is so sincere
To those who look and draw near
Christ our Saviour, the Eternal being
Who died for us to set us free

Do not wait before it is too late
And miss the chance to be great
Secured, redeemed and full of faith
Saved by His amazing grace

We are His, The true beloved
Washed and cleansed from all our flaws
Perfectly, he redeems the thirsty soul
That genuinely seek and worship Him

Jeremiah 31: 3 The LORD appeared to him from afar, saying, "I have loved you with an everlasting love; therefore I have drawn you with lovingkindness"

VALLEY OF HOPE

Let us dwell in the valley of hope
Finding the wisdom to broaden our scope
With the blessing that flows from the Heavenly
slope
Steadily down the mysterious rope

Jesus is faithful and will always bestows
Blessings from heaven that freely flows
Over every believer from long ago
And those who are converted in body and soul

Romans 15:13 *Now the God of hope fill you with all joy and peace in believing, that ye may abound in hope, through the power of the Holy Ghost.*

SPECIALLY CHOSEN

You are chosen and are set free
Special people that bend the knee
To the Saviour who decrees
That if you follow Him you will see
The glorious nature of Christ living in thee

Royal priesthood favoured and blessed
With the Spirit that possess
The power and boldness to express
The wonders of Jesus as you confess
To the mercy and grace that grows as
 you progress

Deuteronomy 14:2 For thou art an holy people unto the LORD thy God, and the LORD hath chosen thee to be a peculiar people unto himself, above all the nations that are upon the earth.

COURAGEOUS

No power on earth can put you down
God can see everything under the sun
In your weakness you are afraid
But you can win because God comes to your
aid

Every problem can be overcome
Seek the answers and do not be glum
Do not fret, just find for a way
To break the shackles off you today

In every situation watch and pray
And by God's wisdom, troubles will fly away
In His grace, you are secure
For He is The Rock that helps you to endure

Deuteronomy 31:6 Be strong and of good courage, do not fear nor be afraid of them; for the LORD your God, He is the One who goes with you.

PROVIDER

Problems clutter people's mind
Stuck in a rut while counting time
Relying on the works of their own hands
Without the wisdom to think things through

While others wallow in fear and doubt
We stand boldly in whom we trust
Knowing Christ is there for us
Making ways so that we are not lost

All our faith and hope rests in Christ the Lord
The Great Provider for all who call
And seek Him diligently with all their heart
Believing as our Shepherd we shall not lack

Romans 8:32 *He that spared not his own Son, but delivered him up for us all, how shall he not with him also freely give us all things?*

GRATITUDE

Perfect Sacrifice for mankind
Healed the sick and cured the blind
Opened ears and released the dumb
So, that we are delivered from Satan's thumb

He shed His blood that we might live
And understand how much He can give
Stripped and whipped and crowned with thorns
Saving us from the terrors of life storms

In return let us come to Him
Like the angels singing the sweetest hymns
Worshipping Jesus Christ who is our King
With gifts of praise His altar bring

*Hebrews 12:28 28 Therefore let us be grateful
for receiving a kingdom that cannot be shaken,
and thus let us offer to God acceptable worship,
with reverence and awe*

BE COMFORTED

There is no one like our Lord
Hail the King who bears our load
Helps us when our hearts feel cold
Shrouds us with His heavy cloak
Of love and protection that freely flows

Yes, Jesus grants open doors
When you come to Him and implore
For His help and truly adore
The One whose love does endure
Because He reigns forevermore

Joshua 1:9 Have not I commanded thee? Be strong and of a good courage; be not afraid, neither be thou dismayed: for the Lord thy God is with thee whithersoever thou goest.

AWESOME MAJESTY

You reign in awesome majesty
Ruling king for all eternity
Rich in mercy, love and grace
Who has taken away our disgrace

Prince of Valour whose blood was shed
On the cross where sin was slain
Healer of our broken souls
In this world where torment rolls

Psalms 96:6 The LORD reigneth, he is clothed with majesty; the LORD is clothed with strength, wherewith he hath girded himself: the world also is stablished, that it cannot be moved.

CHOOSE TO ABIDE

What will happen on that day?
When Jesus comes what will He say?
Faithful servant come this way
Or you have been unfaithful go away

Will you work in the Lord's vineyard?
As someone who played the right card
Or be counted in the graveyard
destined on the course that is hard

Think well before you decide
Whether you will choose to abide
Under the shadow of the Almighty
Or act on the impulses by the demon's
inside you

Mark 16:15 "And he said unto them, Go ye into all the world, and preach the gospel to every creature.

BLESSED BY GOD

Long ago He broke the yoke
Burst your bonds and set you free
Yet you refused to remember Him

Lift your eyes and you will see
His salvation is always there for you
Through the Spirit He sent to you

Ponder on what He has done for you
Made a way when you were shunned
Turned your darkness into light

Why neglect this amazing gift?
Specially given by Christ the King
Who came to earth that you might live
A life of hope blessed by God

*2 Corinthians 9:8 And God is able to bless you
abundantly, so that in all things at all times,
having all that you need, you will abound in
every good work.*

OUR SALVATION

Who are we without the Lord?
Aimless ships on earth dark seas
Foraging for food and joy
In worthless things that turn to dust

Look to Jesus who is our strength
He came to save us and show the way
To peace, eternity and true love
Blessing all are hands have worked

In your troubles, just kneel and pray
Asking God to lead the way
And your breakthrough will surely come
Because you believe In Christ His Son

Colossians 1:19-20 "For God was pleased to have all his fullness dwell in him, and through him to reconcile to himself all things, whether things on earth or things in heaven, by making peace through his blood, shed on the cross.

WORTHY, WORTHY

Worthy, Worthy are you Lord
For you reign in majesty
Praise and honour is your crown
In whom amazing love is always found

We are sinners that you have saved
In our affliction you humbly came
And opened up an eternal way
Sent the Spirit to guide us when we stray

Revelation 5:12 *Saying with a loud voice,
Worthy is the Lamb that was slain to receive
power, and riches, and wisdom, and strength,
and honour, and glory, and blessing.*

INTERCEDE FOR OTHERS

Intercede for others when you pray
In your quiet time every day
God will listen when you say
I am devoted to Christ in every way

Prayer is the Master key
That unlocks door so that we may say
The mercy Christ gives to those who believe
That they are free from the one who deceives

James 5:16 "Therefore confess your sins to each other and pray for each other so that you may be healed. The prayer of a righteous person is powerful and effective."

GOD'S PROTECTION

Stand your ground, do not be knocked down
Or succumb to pressures that are around
Focus on what you can achieve
Leaving what cannot be reached

In your heart lies someone who is not dark
Strong and capable that holds a spark
Given by God to be a warrior
Undefeated because His power is so glorious

Victory in Christ is assured
Once you believe and are reassured
Nothing can harm you and you remain sure
That He will faithfully protect you to the core

Isaiah 54:17 "No weapon that is formed against thee shall prosper; and every tongue that shall rise against thee in judgment thou shalt condemn. This is the heritage of the servants of the LORD, and their righteousness is of me, saith the LORD."

STRENGTH IN GOD

Hope is rest assured
Strong in faith and reassured
That the Lord brings peace on every shore
Though you face battles that is for sure

Nothing can withstand God's mighty power
That arrives within the hour
Breaking chains that wilt like flowers
Burnt alive from heavenly showers

God is able to deliver
Those who trust in Him and not the Deceiver
Given grace because they are believers
Washed and cleansed and are now receivers

Of God's love that spreads with fervour
Stamping out all virulent fevers
Of discontent, fear and bad behaviour
Reconciled through Jesus Christ
who is our Redeemer

1 Thessalonians 1:3 **We remember before our God**
 and Father your work produced by faith, your labour prompted by love, and your endurance inspired by hope in our Lord Jesus Christ.

LOVED BY THE LORD

Who can love us like the Lord?
We are bound to Him with a cord
Living life in one accord
Redeemed, forgiven without discord

He is faithful to the end
He will never lie or pretend
Through His grace we can extend
The peace and joy that has no end

John3 :16 For God so loved the world, that he gave his only begotten Son, that whosoever believeth in him should not perish, but have everlasting life.

GUIDE ME LORD

Guide me Lord, the dark surrounds me
Steal me from the Tempest's grasp
Troubles rage all around me
Fear and dread hold me in its clasp

I am reaching out, please come and
save me
From the pit, I will arise
I see your hand, my hope is rising
As new light comes streaming in

Now, I know He is ever near me
Listens and comes when I call
Freed me from all worldly terrors
Brought me safely to the other side

Psalms 25:5 **Lead me in thy truth and teach me: for thou art the God of my salvation; on thee do I wait all the day.**

LOST FAITH

Have you lost your faith as you surmise
You are worthless and will not rise?
While negative thoughts are building up
in size
Saying that you will never be wise

Jesus came to break all ties
Of depression and failure that sing their
lullabies
That you will remain hopeless covered by
the devil's disguise
Unworthy of the promise that Christ lays
before your eyes

Know that you are priceless, of noble
enterprise
Empowered by the Saviour who rests beyond
the skies
And endowed in God's resplendent glory
In whom you shall arise

1 Peter 5:10 And after you have suffered for a little while, the God of all grace, who has called you to His eternal glory in Christ, will Himself restore you, secure you, strengthen you, and establish you.

GOD'S HOLY ORDER

Jesus promised to always love us
A wedding vow of Christ with us
Brought salvation and took away the curse
With grace abounding and poured out for us

We are brothers, sons and daughters
Included in God's Holy order
Steering us through troubled water
Shielding us within fortified borders

Choose today who you will serve
Forget the past and what you deserve
Be believers that observe
The word of God that you preserve

Romans 5:8 "But God demonstrates his own love for us in this: While we were still sinners, Christ died for us."

INSPIRATION OF OUR LORD

Inspiration from our Lord
Spreads across the land
A perfect message to mankind
Saving souls because He is kind

Out of love for humankind
He sent His only Son to seek and to find
All the lost and broken who need a hand
To be set free from the evil fiend

Let us rejoice and gather near
And see the wonders that become clear
What our Gentle Saviour has already put in
gear
That leads to salvation and grace to sinners
ear

*2 Timothy 3:16 All scripture is given by
inspiration of God, and is profitable for
doctrine, for reproof, for correction, for
instruction in righteousness:*

MERCY SHOWS

Jesus hears us when we call
Picks us up when we fall
Builds our hope so that we stand tall
Beats our foes and makes them fall

We have to let others know
Of the love that He bestows
And the light that brightly glows
In our hearts as His mercy shows

1 John 5:14 **This is the confidence we have in approaching God:** *that* **if we ask anything according to his will, he hears us.**

CHRIST OUR LORD

Let us praise Jesus Christ our Lord
Who is King to us all
He healed the sick and raised the dead
Came to earth, are souls are fed

Reigns triumphantly from the skies
Prepares a place for when we die
Promises that we will come to Him on High
And worship Him forever nigh

Psalms 150:1 Praise ye the Lord. Praise God in his sanctuary: praise him in the firmament of his power.

LIVE AGAIN

Let us praise Jesus Christ our Lord
Who is King to us all
He healed the sick and raised the dead
Came to earth, are souls are fed

Reigns triumphantly from the skies
Prepares a place for when we die
Promises that we will come to Him on High
And worship Him forever nigh

*Philippians 4:4 "Rejoice in the Lord
alway: and again I say, Rejoice."*

MOTHER MARY

Queen of heaven, virgin dear
The perfect vessel for Christ our Lord
Lowly handmaid who bore the Son
Whose immaculate conception changed
the world

Mother Mary meek and mild
Who all ages now call blessed
Chosen to bear a Special child
And in humility passed the test

She stands and mediates on our behalf
Virgin pure who did her part
Showing kindness to all mankind
Helps all sinners to find her Son

Romans16:6 Greet Mary, who bestowed
much labour on us

SON OF MAN

He is the God that changeth not
Who builds the church upon the rock
The unseen God who sent Christ the Son
To be the Saviour, Lord of all the earth

He reigns with power, truth and love
In the world and in Heaven above
The Eternal God, one in three
In His might as the Blessed Trinity

The Son of Man He sent to us
As people question is He the One?
Elijah, Jeremiah or John the Baptist
Or perhaps a Prophet that was foretold

Yet only those who truly hear
Will know that He is the Son of God
The Living God that took our place
And by his death we are reborn

*Matthew 9:6 But so that you may know that the Son of Man has authority on earth to forgive sins"—then He *said to the paralytic, "Get up, pick up your bed and go home."*

RESURRECTION

He is the resurrection and the life
He will give redemption without strife
He will raise you up to new life
Where joy and peace is ever rife

The dry bones rose from out the grave
And death could no longer enslave
Lazarus heard and so was raised
And Martha, Mary sung out their praise

So listen now to those who hear
With the Lord there's hope not fear
It's time to cry and call His name
For that is why He really came

Out of the depths, let's cry to God
To take away this heavy load
He sent His Son to save the unjust
And restore to all what they had lost

*John 11:25-26 Jesus said unto her, I am
the resurrection, and the life: he that
 believeth in me, though he were dead,
yet shall he live: And whosoever liveth
and believeth in me shall never die.
Believest thou this?*

THE VINER

Who am I but a speck of dust?
Moulded in the potter's hand
To be the person that God has found
Kind, obedient that grace surrounds

Drawn according to the Painter's brush
Designed internally and not in a rush
Perfected by the father's masterstroke
God's project that has the fastest growth

Now the rib is a masterpiece
When troubles calm and worries cease
Christ 's foundation on which I am built
A branch dependent on the Viner's gifts

John 15: 1*I am the true vine, and my Father is the husbandman*

FORMIDABLE GOD

You are moving the immovable
And shaking the unshakeable
Proving that you can break the unbreakable
And change the unchangeable

Doing what is impossible
Showing people that all things are possible
Breaking chains that were impenetrable
Proving that your love is incredible

Showing wonders that are unforgettable
Making His power accessible
Doing what is incomprehensible
As proof that He is formidable

Deuteronomy 3:24 *O Lord GOD, thou hast begun
to shew thy servant thy greatness, and
thy mighty hand: for what God is there in
heaven or in earth, that can do according to thy
works, and according to thy might?*

SELF BELIEF

Why are you wondering which way to go?
As you let your worries flow
Letting fear and despair within you grow
And your trust in God drops to a low

There is a way that you may know
To let the light within you glow
You have a choice to serve a blow
On indecision, failure and being slow

Place your trust in God who long ago
Sent His Son so that we will know
How much love that He bestows
On those who surrender to the Spirit now

*2 Corinthians 1:9 In fact, we expected to die.
But as a result, we stopped relying on
ourselves and learned to rely only on God, who
raises the dead.*

CELESTIAL BEINGS

Many feel the mounting pain
constantly under the fate of strain
Jesus came to maintain
A life that is free of unseen chains

There is a longing in our hearts
To sweetly sing and be a part
Of your great love that always lasts
And leads you onto an eternal path

Worship him the Kings of Kings
Sing in adoration on cherubic wings
Sovereign power flow from heavens
springs
Enjoyed by every celestial beings

Psalm 103:20 Bless the LORD, ye his angels, that excel in strength, that do his commandments, hearkening unto the voice of his word.

LOVE YOUR NEIGHBOUR

Fleeting though our life may be
There is time for all to see
The Child of God that lives in thee
Following Christ in works and deeds

Love your neighbour as yourself
With care and devotion there is nothing left
For we know that by good works
We stand a chance to reach Heaven's door

Mark 12:30-31 And thou shalt love the Lord thy God with all thy heart, and with all thy soul, and with all thy mind, and with all thy strength: this is the first commandment. And the second is like, namely this, Thou shalt love thy neighbour as thyself. There is none other commandment greater than these.

COME DISCIPLES

Broken cords, broken chains
Removed all barriers of disdain
Took away lasting shame
Changed our lives, gave us a new name

Then He said "Come disciples follow Me
I will be a light unto thee
Replace your darkness with thoughts of Me
And fill your life with grace that is free"

"I am faithful, and I am true
I will guide and see you through
Every trial that comes your way
I am near so do not fear
For I am Christ that dwells in you"

*Matthew 28:19 Go ye therefore, and teach all
nations, baptizing them in the name of the
Father, and of the Son, and of the Holy Ghost*

HIS PROMISE

Walk in the light that shineth bright
Warming those that come to the light
Jesus stands for us in the spiritual fight
And takes us up to the greatest height

He sent the Spirit to open our hearts
Guide us through the darkened path
Save us from the forthcoming wrath
And gives us victory over every evil dart

*1 Kings 8:56 Blessed be the L*ORD*, that hath given rest unto his people Israel, according to all that he promised: there hath not failed one word of all his good promise, which he promised by the hand of Moses his servant.*

PATIENT GOD

There is no one like our God
Loving and kind no matter what
Saviour in whose thoughts are just
Forgiving us from our worldly lusts

He is our Shepherd guiding us
Solid foundation in whom we trust
Gathering every soul that is lost
 and leads us on the path to righteousness

2 Thessalonians 3:5 And the Lord direct your
hearts into the love of God, and into
the patient waiting for Christ.

TRUST IN JESUS

In Jesus we have come to trust
And overcome the devil's thrust
 Christ has taken away distrust
That held us like victims that are trussed

We are among the Chosen ones
Travelling to a place above the Sun
Where the angels live and, in their song,
Praise the Lord in different tongues

2 Samuel 22:31 As for God, his way is perfect; the word of the LORD is tried: he is a buckler to all them that trust in him.

CHOSEN RACE

Rejoice, there is no more shame
Jesus came and changed your name
Now you are not the same
Freed from every form of blame

Jesus in His amazing way
Has taken your thorns away
Moulding you into a pot of clay
Designed to act in His special play

You are part of God's chosen race
He has gone to prepare a place
Where you will dance with heavenly grace
And you are welcomed into His embrace

1 Peter 2:9 But ye are a chosen generation, a royal priesthood, an holy nation, a peculiar people; that ye should shew forth the praises of him who hath called you out of darkness into his marvellous light;

GOD'S GRACE

Can you see what the Lord has done?
Through the darkness he brought out the sun
Made us free and burdens light
Brought us hope that is burning bright

Breaking boulders that stand in your way
Cleared the path so that you will say
"Master Jesus who has come today
To lead me out of death's deadly rays"

Ephesians 2:8-9 For by grace are ye saved through faith; and that not of yourselves: it is the gift of God: Not of works, lest any man should boast.

HOLY, HOLY IS OUR GOD

Holy, Holy, Holy is our God
Who leads and owns the whole Universe
Existed before time began
Created us and called us man

Mighty Saviour to all mankind
Gentle, loving and very kind
Protecting us from the evil one
Victorious in battles won

He is Master of eternity
Great Redeemer whose love is king
Shelter for the lost, forsaken ones
Healer and Deliverer of the chosen ones

*Isaiah 6:3 And one cried unto another, and
said, Holy, holy, holy, is the Lord of hosts: the
whole earth is full of his glory.*

WONDERS OF THE LORD

In any affliction, call on His name
Who has taken away your shame
Made your enemies inane
Broke the chains for your gain

Low and worthless you may feel
There is more than your eyes can see
Behold the wonders of the Lord
Flowing down to reach to you

*Psalms 77:11 I will remember thy works
of the Lord: surely, I will remember thy
 wonders of old*

CHRIST OUR CONQUEROR

By His grace you are set free
And in His name you can decree
Demons fall and trouble flee
Bringing evil to its knees

Wield the strength that dwells in you
By the power that Jesus gave to you
Put the devil under your shoe
And Christ will fight every battle that faces you

Romans 8:37 Nay, in all these things we are more than conquerors through him that loved us.

OUR FOUNDATION

Jesus Christ the burning light
That shines so bright in the darkened night
Drives away our doubts and fears
Ever near with a listening ear

The Prince of Peace who's radiance glows
And fills the heart with hope that grows
Frees the captives and those oppressed
Gives them life because they are blessed

Clothed and decked in glorious sheen
Crowned with joy with a heavenly theme
Born of love from our God above
Whose living water is like a treasure trove

Matthew 7:24 Therefore whosoever heareth these sayings of mine, and doeth them, I will liken him unto a wise man, which built his house upon a rock

PEACE WITH THE SPIRIT

Many carry the cross of stress
Never asking for redress
Flailing like a drowning man
Swallowed whole before their race began

Circumstances push and then they follow
 it leaves them feeling sad and hollow
Rise and fight because there is hope tomorrow
Time to shake off fear and sorrow

Stand up tall and realise
Things can change before your eyes
There is no room for compromise
You have an Angel in disguise

Invite the Spirit, the Holy One
Who drives away the evil one
 He makes those problems go away
And gives you peace that will always stay

1 Peter 5:7 Casting all your care upon him; for he careth for you.

DELIVERED

Never let the worries come
And take away your peace and joy
In your troubles, just stop and think
Jesus came and made a way

On your knees, look up and say
Great Provider, the Holy One
Give me all I need today
And let your wisdom guide me every day

He is faithful and He is just
Supplies your needs, in who you trust
To break the chains that are unjust
And bring you freedom at no extra cost

Genesis 14:20 And blessed be the Most High God, which hath delivered thine enemies into thy hand. And he gave him tithes of all.

SAVED

You are hurting in the shadows
And your heart feels dark and fallow
Wondering when life will take a turn
And drive away the fears that churn

Reaching out for a helping hand
Searching for a friend or band
That will take the pain away
And open up a brand-new way

Hope will surely make a way
Blotting out what is dim and grey
Love will come and break the chain
Through Jesus Christ, who is the way

Keep your worries far away
Look and see what is on its way
Let Jesus come and have His say
Show you mercy that is here to stay

You are saved, redeemed, delivered
A part of God's illustrious plan

Ephesians 2:8-9 For by grace are
ye saved through faith; and that not of
yourselves: it is the gift of God: Not of works,
lest any man should boast.

HE CALLS TO YOU

Jesus Christ the burning light
That shines so bright in the darkened night
Drives away our doubts and fears
Ever near with a listening ear

The Prince of Peace who's radiance glows
And fills the heart with hope that grows
Frees the captives and those oppressed
Gives them life because they are blessed

Clothed and decked in glorious sheen
Crowned with joy with a heavenly theme
Born of love from our God above
Whose living water is like a treasure trove

1 Corinthians 1:26 For ye see your calling, brethren, how that not many wise men after the flesh, not many mighty, not many noble, are called:

THE MISSION

Give thanks to the Holy One
Whose love shines like the morning sun
Blowing across the Promised land
With the message of Salvation to those
 who will understand

All power belongs to Jesus Christ
Whose mission is to save those in His sight
He is the reason why we are alive
Who kindles love that never dies

Let us place our trust in Him
He is the one who went out on a limb
To become man that we may find
Eternal life, leaving sin behind

*Colossians 3:23 And whatsoever ye do,
 do it heartily, as to the Lord, and not unto men*

BOUNDLESS GRACE

Though the storm clouds blot the sky
Fear is removed because of Christ
For we know He is close to us
Guiding us through every fight

In our hearts we stand secure
Because we are covered by boundless grace
Let us place our trust in Him
Defender, Protector of living beings

So, in song our voices raise
In triumph of what He has done
Redeemed our souls from the rejected one
With a chance to be like Him

*Ephesians 2:8-9 For by grace are ye saved
through faith; and that not of yourselves: it is the
gift of God*

JESUS CALLS

Can you hear him when He calls?
Though you stumble and you fall
Lost, confused in time and space
Looking for that special place

Listen to the master's voice
Now is the time to make a choice
He is the Shepherd that saves the lost
Paid the price at a heavy cost

Open doors that were once closed
Took away burdens that were imposed
Follow Him and you will see
The beauty of the grace you will receive

1 Corinthians 1:9 God is faithful, by whom ye were called unto the fellowship of his Son Jesus Christ our Lord.

LIGHT THE WAY

Living God who comes to us
Paschal lamb, Pascal bread
Wash away our evil thoughts
Purge all obstacles that sin has brought

Light the way that we may see
The truth in being close to thee
Let our pathway lead to you
Humbled by your words that are true

May the Holy Spirit takes its place
Flow across the human race
Reach inside and change our hearts
And make us worthy to get to the Holy place

John 14:6 "Jesus saith unto him, I am the way, the truth, and the life: no man cometh unto the Father, but by me."

SACRED HEART

Sacred heart pierced for our transgressions
Died so that we could gain admission
By letting our sins fall into remission
And become a part of God's new division

He came to save us from pain and misery
Our light and our Visionary
Pulling down the strongholds with His artillery
And turning back our history

Boldly standing with the breastplate of
Salvation
Filled in the anticipation
That He will fulfil our expectation
Of grace and love unto the next generation

1 Thessalonians 5:8 But let us, who are of the day, be sober, putting on the breastplate of faith and love; and for an helmet, the hope of salvation

GUARDIANS

Defenceless Lambs we may be
Worried by what we see
Uncomprehending thoughts that can be
Thorns of agony in the life you see

Jesus came to set you free
Release you from the pain you feel
Open doors so that you will see
The beauty of His love revealed

He is the Guardian of your soul
Who will restore and make you whole
Slow things down so that you control
What you do and what the future holds

*John 8:36 If the Son therefore shall make
you free, you shall be free*

A WORTHY CHOICE

Mighty Jesus who can compare
To your beauty and your majesty
Loving brother, Lord and Son
Came to earth as the Righteous one

Greater understanding is what we seek
As we follow Christ by being meek
No more outcasts or called freaks
And discounted for being weak

We are victors because of Him
Redeemed, delivered by Christ our King
Living life as He has deemed
Worthy followers that must succeed

1 Peter 1: 3 *"Blessed* be *the God and Father of our Lord Jesus Christ, which according to his abundant mercy hath begotten us again unto a lively hope by the resurrection of Jesus Christ from the dead,*

LOVING KINDNESS

From the depths of sin and darkness
Jesus rose and took away our sadness
Gave us hope through His forgiveness
Restored us to joy and eternal gladness

We proclaim that even in our weakness
That our lives shine with God's own brightness
No more sheltered or blighted by our madness
Freed and loved by God's loving kindness

Colossian 3:12 Put on therefore, as the elect of God, holy and beloved, bowels of mercies, kindness, humbleness of mind, meekness, long suffering

CHRIST OUR KING

Let us trust in Christ our King
Who has made us earthly kins
Made a way so that we will see
The beauty of being set free

No more sorrow, no more grief
Turn to Him and find relief
Before it is time to go to sleep
Forgotten by the world and you sink so deep

1 Corinthians 1:30
*But by His doing you are in Christ Jesus, who
became to us wisdom from God, and
righteousness and sanctification, and
redemption*

MERCIFUL JESUS

Faith is when you believe
In something hoped for not yet seen
Do not let worries weigh you down
Challenges come and then they go

Nothing ever stays the same
Change is constant while we remain
Uncertain at which road to take
Or what tomorrow will bring our way

Trust your instincts, trust your mind
Strive to do the best you can
Call on Jesus and you will see
He is merciful and there for you

Deuteronomy 4: 31 For the Lord thy God is a merciful God; he will not forsake thee, neither destroy thee nor forget the covenant of they fathers which he sware unto them

HOLY FLAMES

When we believed in your name
You came and took away our shame
Broke every chain, things are not the same
Holding on to promises as to heaven claim

Now, we rejoice because He took away all
blame
Overpowering our weakness and earthly pain
delivered us from everything that will cause us
strain
Replacing it with peace that the Lord ordained

So, we make our boast in Jesus' name
Nothing can harm us while we are in His frame
Freely, devoutly living without disdain
Working tirelessly in His Holy flame

*Psalms 34:2 My soul shall make its boast in the
Lord, the humble shall hear and be glad*

WORRIES

Death fired a fatal blow
but Jesus came and brought a glow
Of hope where blessings freely flows
And lights the way that clearly shows
The path to life on which our faith should grow

Trust in God and have no fear
Jesus Christ is always near
 holds you close because you are dear
Fights your battles no matter how severe
And makes your worries disappear

Psalms 56:4 In God I will put my trust, I will praise his word, in God I have put my trust; I will not fear what flesh can do to me

THE WAY

Jesus is the only way
Eagerly waiting to hear you say
Save me Saviour when I stray
Understand me when I display
 actions that should drive you away

Come and rescue me my Lord
Pull me up with your Holy cord
Help me overcome any discord
Fight my battles and in one accord
Let my voice rise with sweetened chords

Singing Master who showers us with great
rewards
In your mercy may we receive awards
Of your love and grace which He has poured
On those who follow and obey, responding
to the Master 's call

Psalm 96:1 - "Sing praise to the Lord, for he has done great things." We are to sing to the Lord because of the great things that the Lord has done for us

GOD'S FLEET

The man you see is no more there
He has evolved and has come to share
His experience and how he dared
Breach humanity because he cared

Thirty-three years he spent on earth
Teaching others how to search
For true freedom and the new church
That leads to Salvation and a rebirth

Come and join in the great feast
Be transformed from the least
Saved from the clutches of the Beast
Now a part of God's own special fleet

*Colossian 3:15 "Let the peace of Christ rule
in your hearts, since as members of one body
you were called to peace. And be thankful."*

SHINING KNIGHT

As you wander through the night
In search of hope and the light
To relieve the pressures that ignite
Fear and dead that blight your sight

Look to Jesus all dressed in white
Who is ready for the fight
And will redeem you from your plight
Save your soul and make things right

He is faithful, make Him your delight
And your life will be quite bright
So, trust In Jesus, your Shining knight
And let hope arise in you like a kite

2 Timothy 1:10 but now has been revealed by the appearing of our Saviour Christ Jesus, who abolished death and brought life and immortality to light through the gospel,

BEYOND BELIEF

Let us sing to Christ our King
Who created everything
For His glory so that we might see
The beauty of being set free

We are sinners yet we believe
That when we place our trust in Thee
And follow all His decrees
We are blessed beyond belief

So, we come as one with you
Relying on the things you do
To inspire, save and see us through
The worst, the best and all that is true

Isaiah 62:11 The Lord has sent out word to the end of the earth, Say to the daughter of Zion, See, your saviour comes; those whom he has made free are with him, and those to whom he has given salvation go before him.

CERTAINTY

He is the Shepherd who stands at the door
Waiting and listening till you answer His call
To follow His footsteps and bow and adore
Jesus our Saviour whose mercy endures

He loves us so much that He came in our place
Carrying our burdens and worldly disgrace
Broke every chain that held us in sin
Gave us a chance set at begin

Your fortunes are turning as the tide rolls on
Bringing you hope at the break of the dawn
Light in the darkness from where you came
from
Giving you victory over what has now gone

Hebrews 13:20 Now may the God of peace— who brought up from the dead our Lord Jesus, the great Shepherd of the sheep, and ratified an eternal covenant with his blood

NOT DONE

When you think that you are alone
With no more fight and you are done
Listen to the voice knocking at your door
Saying I have come like I did before

Bruised and broken, you feel despair
And you feel that no one cares
Understand who looks at your affairs
While you are kneeling in prayer

Jesus comes when you are unaware
Changing destiny while you sit and stare
Showing you that He is always there
Reminding you of the cross He bears

1 Timothy 2:5: For there is one God, and one mediator between God and men, the man Christ Jesus

OPEN DOORS

Many roads seem dark and bleak
Shadows cast even from the peak
Doubt and shame face you all week
And you are desperate and feel weak

Look to Jesus who upon the cross
Bore your pain, took away your loss

Through His death, paid at a cost
You are redeemed, no longer lost

There is no one quite like our Lord
Who is able to restore
Fame and fortune from his Holy store
And open up those closed doors

*1 Chronicle 29:11 Yours, Lord, is the greatness
and the power and the glory and the majesty
and the splendour, for everything in heaven and
earth is yours. Yours, Lord, is the kingdom; you
are exalted as head over all*

HOLY SPIRIT

Holy Spirit come and burn bright
Ignite in us your white light
shielding us in the fight
From shame and everything that would blight
The power of Christ who has made right
Life on earth in God's own sight

Let the outpouring of the Holy Spirit
Bring anointing and inherit
The gift of tongues given not by merit
But as grace for the Lord's own credit
Saving souls who will hear it
And preach the word that comes from it

John 14:26 **But the Comforter, which is the Holy Ghost, whom the Father will send in my name, he shall teach you all things, and bring all things to your remembrance, whatsoever I have said unto you**.

REDEMPTION STORY

This is the day of salvation
For those who welcome Me
It is the Lord your Saviour
Who is reaching out to you

Remember who you are
I died to set you free
Released you from your bondage
And gave you a brand-new name

Bruised and badly beaten
Stripped and then cast out
A cross was what they gave Me
To carry to My grave

This is the Redemption story
Perfected by my death
Where sin has been forgiven
And captives have been set free

Titus 2:14 **Who gave himself for us, that he might redeem us from all iniquity, and purify unto himself a peculiar people, zealous of good works**.

HAVE FAITH

By the power of His name
Demons bow in disarray
Releasing man from guilt and shame
Bringing light with shining rays
Showing us that He loves us still

Who can wrestle with the Lord?
Or change the destiny He ordained?
Do not waver in your faith
He protects everyone that believes
That He is able to save their souls

You are blessed so do not fear
What the devil is out to do
Look to Jesus who is always there
Grant you solace when you fall
And deliver you when you call

1 Corinthians 16:13
Be watchful, stand firm in the faith, act
like men, be strong

BE ENCOURAGED

Why do you worry about tomorrow?
Wallowing in needless sorrow
Wondering when the terrors come
And steal away your joy

Do not be afraid, your answer is on its way
Blessed in the assurance that Jesus has the
say
you are not forsaken, lost or gone astray
For He is the loving shepherd that shelters
you every single day
Simply trust in Him

*Matthew 6:34 Therefore do not worry about
tomorrow, for tomorrow will worry about itself.
Each day has enough trouble of its own.*

A WORTHY CHOICE

Mighty Jesus who can compare
To your beauty and your majesty
Loving brother, Lord and Son
Came to earth as the Righteous one
Greater understanding is what we seek
As we follow Christ by being meek
No more outcasts or called freaks
And discounted for being weak

We are victors because of Him
Redeemed, delivered by Christ our King
Living life as He has deemed
Worthy followers that must succeed

James 1:17 Every good and perfect gift is from above, coming down from the Father of the heavenly lights, who does not change like shifting shadows.

BITTER SWEET

 No matter how bittersweet our life can be
Jesus changes what we feel and see
He is the one who will set us free
Make us greater than we believe

Hope is the gift He freely gives
And builds our faith that we might live
Holy, acceptable in all we do
Walking in the ways we are expected to

1 John 5:13-14 I write these things to you who believe in the name of the Son of God that you may know that you have eternal life. And this is the confidence that we have toward him, that if we ask anything according to his will he hears us.

Author's Note

We are all free in Christ. I pray that this collection of poems will reach into the hearts of its readers exemplifying the fact that we were once lost but by the love and grace bestowed upon us through the Blood of Christ poured out for us all, we are Saved.

Ephesians 1:7 In whom we have our redemption through his blood, the forgiveness of our trespasses, according to the riches of his grace.